**Even The Slightest Touch
Thunders on My Skin**

Even The Slightest Touch Thunders On My Skin

Lorraine Gane

Black Moss Press
2002

Copyright © Lorraine Gane 2002

Published by Black Moss Press at 2450 Byng Road, Windsor, Ontario N8W 3E8. Black Moss books are distributed in Canada and the U.S. by Firefly Books, 3680 Victoria Park Ave., Willowdale, Ont. Canada. All orders should be directed there.

Black Moss would like to acknowledge the generous support of the Canada Council and the Ontario Arts Council for its publishing program.

National Library of Canada Cataloguing in Publication

Gane, Lorraine, 1953-
    Even the slightest touch thunders on my skin / Lorraine Gane.

Poems.
ISBN 0-88753-366-3
    I. Title.
PS8563.A5759E84 2002   C811'.6
C2002-903043-9
PR9199.4.G36E84 2002

*This book is in memory
of Greg Doherty*

Table of Contents

QUESTIONS
Out of This We Must Live   9

DOORS
The Doctor's Office   23
Faces   24
The House of Hope and Death   25
Angel of the Waters   29
Interlude   30

THE STILL POINT
Falling   33
Vigil   34
Wave   40

IN THE DEPTHS
The Box   43
Blessings   45
Descent: Crossing the Dream   46
The Birthday   55
Conversations with a Dead Man   56
Letters From Him   57
Undeciphered Oracle   58

LIGHT
Silence Gathering in Blue Air   62

NOTES   63
ACKNOWLEDGEMENTS   65

QUESTIONS

...try to love the questions themselves like locked rooms and like books that are written in a very foreign tongue. Do not now seek the answers, which cannot be given you because you would not be able to live them. And the point is, to live everything. Live the questions now. Perhaps you will then gradually, without noticing it, live along some distant day into the answer

—Rainer Maria Rilke

Out of This We Must Live

1. The white bed

Then,
the unknown broke deep in us.
Men in white cloth illuminated
a box on the wall.
The white space on the film
was the thing growing in you.
Now hope means lying on a white bed,
clear liquid running into your hand—
this is the plan of action.
Still, they don't know what's growing in you.
Man-eating fetus crawling
up the tail of your spine

2. Questions

Why has this happened to you?
When did you let the darkness creep into the hollow
of your back?
Who will chart the bone-white
skin between my thighs
on mornings after dawn enters through your window?
Who will speak to your mother on winter days
when the sky mourns the sun's absence and we cannot
see the pearl light of the moon?
Will you sit in the garden next summer under the growing
hands of the old maple tree?
Will you ever again
wrap your maleness around my shoulders
like a cloak of radiant light?

.Princess Margaret's Hospital

St. Valentine's and I've brought you
a card, video and two ripe mangoes.
I pull these from my purse in the washroom,
straighten my red wool dress with gold buttons
—I want to look my best—then enter the hall
to your room smelling of chicken soup and
sweet forsythia blooms. On the bed,
mouth curling into a smile, a quick kiss
on the cheek brings you to your feet
in sheepskin slippers, arms around me.
"I've a present for you," you say.
"Close your eyes and hold out your hands."
I ready myself, anticipating the promised
chocolates on my tongue. Something
goes into my hand. Eyes open,
I see a lump of white tissue spotted
with tiny red hearts. Inside is a banana.
"I couldn't go shopping," you grin
like a boy caught in a mischievous act.
"I'm sorry, I gave the chocolates
to my mother." I hide my disappointment,
smiling. Soon your arms are around me
again, dissolving my sadness and
everything else in the room—
the wires on your arms, the bottles
of liquid on poles, the florescent
lights overhead. We're somewhere far away
in a warm pool playing like children
on their first summer day from school.

The water sparkles in your eyes,
on your skin, in your hair. It sprays
around us as we become water, sky,
sun. Suddenly, I look up.
A nurse is aiming
a thermometer in your ear

4. Dream I

It is midday under a grey sky.
Through a grove of trees
on a large rock
a woman with eyes the color of snow
lies half-naked flailing her arms
and legs screaming, "No, No!"
Beside her a muscular man
with a black hood over his face
raises a mallet in the air
and with all his force
slams it down on the woman.
From a hook hanging
above the woman is a man's torso,
without arms, legs or head.
I recognize you—
the woman on the rock is me

5. The next time

You're sleeping soundly at last
your face soft and innocent against the covers.
A plastic pail rests on the floor
waiting for the next time.
We can never tell when that will be.
We must be ready to bring your head forward
steady over the rim,
hands on your trembling back as the green river
flows from your mouth.
Soon, the sun will lift into the sky
and when the light comes dancing
over the white waves in the yard
you'll open your eyes and smile.
I'll bring you tea and mangoes
and you will slice clean the flesh from the pits.
I will watch you take each slice into your mouth
close your eyes and wait till the sweet yellow
dissolves in the praise of your tongue

6. Parts taken

This is not the body you wanted me to have
you say, clasping a belt around folds of your pants
half-naked in front of the mirror
searching for parts taken by the clear liquid,
the test of your strength now measured in how much you
can squeeze your willow arms around me.
As the months go by your face chisels
into its beauty—polished cheekbones,
eyes sunken, holding new light

7. "Protective Isolation"

Down the hall of closed doors the curtains are drawn,
except for this one, "Protective isolation."
Bodies huddle beside the door, the men in dark suits and ties,
the young girl with pigtails in a blue dress.
A large-boned woman beside a white bed feeds
a thin figure upright over a tray.
I cannot tell if it is a man or woman.
I see only a snow-white head, eyes sunken
like those of Nazi prisoners, staring
at the large woman's hand raising a spoon in the air

8. Night

In the half-dark room you sit cross-legged
on the bed: a moon man glowing silver
over sheer skin, eyes small valleys, lips lizard thin.
You are all hard lines and angles
but softness pours through your fingers
etching a secret language
over my breasts
and I think this may be all there is,
this moment on a winter's night
when even the slightest touch
thunders on my skin.
Later, in the hour before dawn
I wake to your eyes wide and pensive,
your hand opening my lips with a crescent of orange,
voice whispering in my ear:
"You slept through my kisses"

9. Dream III

Early morning, you wake from a dream:
in a room you sit with a man wearing blue pajamas
and a white wristband. Slowly, his lips turn into a smile,
his bony fingers offering a cup of Javex. You refuse.
The walls close in, a door opens, you run down a hill
of flowers that turn into garbage bags.
You climb over a wall of tin cans
that turn into dog food. Men with shiny heads
bend over a table selling pistachio nuts
that become plastic ears in your hands.
"Nothing is as it seems," you say in the dark,
pillow wet with tears

10. I kiss your lips

On your breath
I inhale mercury, cheek hot against my skin,
your eyes growing deep into the bones of your face,
and it is the present I want now,
even the single tear down your cheek,
the greyness gathering in your eyes,
arms like a boy's,
hand clenching mine as you say:
"Soon I'll be the man you met"

11. The return

The room at the end of the hall is dark.
I walk into grainy air and draw the curtain.
You lay in bed, covers over your head.
I call your name and slowly you emerge,
skin swollen and green, eyes an overcast sky.
"Where have you been?" I want to ask.
Was it what the doctor said, numbers too high?"
I don't ask these questions.
Instead, I kiss your cheek, help you dress.
A friend lifts you into the wheelchair.
We are bringing you home

January - April, 1993
Toronto

DOORS

...you must believe and not believe
that door you came in you must go out again

–Jan Zwicky

The Doctor's Office

We wait in the lounge till your name
is called, then take our places
in the small room—your mother and I
on chairs, you on the table,
rocking back and forth,
your mouth open like a fish.
Any moment now you will throw up,
I think, but the doctor comes in
and perches his long thin body
on the ledge against the wall.
I watch as he shifts his weight,
then tells us the thing is still growing
in you, though we are not without hope.
There's a new drug from the Yew tree—
last resort is a bone marrow transplant.
His words shoot across the room
like a rain of needles,
stabbing the surface of my skin
then burrowing into muscles underneath.
Your mother's face is now as white
as her starched shirt. You stop rocking.
Your low voice answers the doctor's questions,
then he leaves to call New York,
where new treatments begin in a week.
By the time he closes the door,
sharp pins break through
the skin of my heart

Faces

I cannot look at my face any more.
When I hold the small mirror to eyes
rivered in red lines with sleep
still waiting, I see a white bed,
your eyes like stones the morning you woke
to a blurred room, fearing you were going blind.

I cannot look at my hair any more.
For months, I've tied it back, reined in
its urge to spread thick over my shoulders
so unlike the sheen you now wear,
white head gleaming.

I cannot look at my lips any more.
My lips lead me to your mouth that first
time, wet and wandering in the darkened car,
a dream loosened in the months that followed.
Now we kiss on the cheek.
Germs breed in the mouth,
be careful, the white bed takes back
the wanderers

The House of Hope and Death

On the sidewalk
bodies with bald heads
slouch in wheelchairs,
cigarettes in one hand,
IVs dripping into the other.
They smile with stained teeth
as I pass into the glass doors.
Upstairs,
you lean towards me
in a pool of white light
skin the color of snow
even your eyelashes seared.
Tears at the edges of your eyes
fall into the swell of my hands

*

Days stretch out in light from your window
the Hudson curling below in grey mist
the sound of sirens dissolving
in the thick July heat.
No one told us you'd end up
a living ghost
inching your way back to color

*

Sleepless nights.
Rawness grows deep in your body
till there is nothing left
but a large space
where dark voices speak

You, who are not religious,
send for a priest.
Nothing he says helps.
Only tears release
the broken shards
from your eyes

*

I'm surviving on air
breathing in this world
and another
in rooms where white coats come and go,
hooded eyes watching this human experiment,
clipboards full of numbers
charting the ebb and flow
of wanton cells.
Twenty years from now
they'll call this barbaric.
Your bones will speak
of marrow pilfered and frozen
blood burnt
with cobalt and mercury

*

Your eyes are dark pools
I enter in the night
bringing my bag of bones and branches
to the landing where I seek
the light you carry in your palms.
I come without maps or plans
all those things I give to my days.

I come naked,
to be filled up.

*

You tell me what I don't want to hear:
Death spoke and you listened
for an instant
your head over the yellow pail,
the night long and sleepless
hour after hour
pressing down on the door
of the room
where darkness waits
like a hungry dog
for a scrap of food

*

They tell us we were not meant to suffer
but we fell from grace
our wings smashing on the rocks,
blood and bones
into the earth.
What is the meaning of this?
Surely something must
come from this pain

*

The voices fill the room with numbers,
cheer painted on phrases
rehearsed in other rooms like these:
"the prognosis is good,
you are not like the others"

*

Behind the walls,
the voices of the dead cry out,
but I do not listen to them.
I hear cries down the hall,
a child waiting for the doctors
to cut the cancer from his face.
I hear the man's voice
behind the orange curtain,
a year to live and he speaks
the same two Russian words
day after day
when the doctor asks how he feels.
I hear
the slow heave of your heart
sounding its quiver in my ears

*

This is not what I wanted:
These nights on the narrow bed
singing to the walls
these days walking silent halls
these moments watching you sleep
like a small child
cradled away from his goblins.
Hope is a long journey
through the house of death

Angel of the Waters

I don't know why
I stand here watching
her brown gleaming body
above the fountain
in Central Park.

I scan her face
for some slight smile
some wink in her eye
something to let me know she
is watching me too.

The sight of her wings
open and ready
to take her up
into the clear blue sky
makes me think
I too can fly
back to the room
six blocks east
to touch your cooling hand
as you fall
further and further
into the last sleep

Interlude

I'm surprised at how you glide through
the crowds with such ease,
eat the raison buns with gusto
walking the wide paths
of Central Park only stopping
by a pond to let me rest.

But then you always surprise me.
Back in the room folded on the bed
you are slow wind sharing your secrets
in the fading light of an August afternoon

THE STILL POINT

...at the still point, there the dance is.
But neither arrest nor movement. And do not call it fixity,
from nor towards.
Neither ascent nor decline. Except for the point, the still point,
There would be no dance, and there is only the dance

—T. S. Eliot

Falling

On the way to
the downstairs room
with no phones or pictures
you say you'll be all right.

That night I dream I am moving
into high waves slamming
my face, eyes closed.

I hold a rope tied
to the boat that will
take me up the Hudson
to your room,
tubes breathing air
pumping blood
wires to your heart.

Dawn. A bird on the highest
branch watches other birds
swooping in the air, waiting
for the news of the day

Vigil

How can it come to this?
The room—grey, pulsing with screens
flashing red and green
plastic bags of liquids on poles.
The body—mouth with tubes
breathing air
legs and arms propped on pillows,
eyes glued shut with Vaseline.
For days I stand mute,
unable to step through the wall of silence
into the space you've become

*

The nurse says what the doctors won't:
"Deterioration...not processing...
white cells too low."
I run out to the street
hot pavement under my feet
walking blindly
the air thick with sun.
Somehow, I find myself
in a courtyard of green
cool marble under my thighs.
In the ferns a bronzed angel points
a thin finger over my shoulder
to a closed door

*

You come in a dream
face smiling
sitting in your blue robe
on the edge of the bed.
You say:
"I wait in blue spaces,
soft breezes fill my lungs
under the sun.
I want to tell you
about the light in your eyes,
the oceans I see there,
the tides stretching farther and farther
from the shore."
Night falls.
The moon wakes,
a shimmer of hope
slips behind the clouds

*

The doors of your heart are closing,
heavy with fungus, says the doctor
and one more bag is added to the fifteen
swinging over your bed.
Now your chest
moves in a new rhythm.
It lifts and falls into a flutter
as though something inside
wants to escape

*

The nurse hooks
a plastic hose to your mouth,
maroon liquid shoots
into the tall glass by the bed.
I shut my eyes
against muffled coughing
and the sound of sucking air

*

You wake from a deep sleep
head bolting forward
eyes wide
peering through a liquid sheen
hand reaching
through the air.
I know you want to speak
but your lips cannot part.
As you look through me
a black snake
coils around my throat
choking my words.
Now the nurse is beside us
her voice a soft wind.
She asks:
"Do you want the blinds down?"
"Are you in pain?"
You shake your head,
a small child
falling back to his dreams

*

I sit by the window watching you,
book on my lap,
letters by Myrtle Fillmore
whose tuberculosis vanished
after months of prayer.
Her words bathe me
but my prayers for you
seem wasted.
Over and over
I've asked God for a cure
but I see no change.
You've lain here
for nearly twelve days,
slipping ever more deeply
into the last sleep

*

Three of us are in the room.
I hold one hand, your mother the other.
A long-time friend
stands guard at your feet.
You are a wisp of breath, a golden thread
in the seesaw of machine air.
My lips on your hand
etch its memory forever in my mind:
skin a perfect pinkness,
nails of two moons on each finger,
palms like silk

*

The waiting room is dark
except for the yellow glow from the hall
where footsteps wake me from a dream:
I'm swimming in a blue-green ocean
towards your boat
sinking
down into the darkening waters,
my hand on the bowring
lifting you up
as I rise to the surface
breathing
then sinking down again into the dark
my arms full of stones.
I must let go
or drown

*

Mid-afternoon. I come to your room
ready to speak.
The nurse pulls down
the bed rail,
pushes the wires and tubes
to one side,
closes the door.
Slowly,
I raise up to the bed,
lay my head on your chest
speaking softly in your ear,
confessing my need to save you,
hold you here with us,
even against God's will

*

The room shatters
with wailing from the screen
I jump to my feet,
leap to your bed
Your chest rises and falls
once more, then stops

September, 1993
New York City

Wave

He is lifted
into the wave
of his last breath,
the body on the bed
turning white,
hands, legs
dissolving
into the light,
white lotus
opening to the sky,
the star
he becomes

IN THE DEPTHS

The Box

This is no ordinary box.
A container the size of a hat,
wrapped in brown paper, neatly taped,
the box sits between his mother and me,
small and inconspicuous.
Six weeks before, I brought him to New York
in a body—six feet, a hundred and ninety
pounds of lively male flesh. Now all we have
left of him is this box.
His mother's white liquid eyes
tell me she, too, cannot understand
this sudden transformation.
I cover her hand with mine over the box
jolting from the seat as the taxi
careens through traffic.
At the airport, we place the box
into a brown leather bag.
His mother carries it through X-ray.
At home, she sets the contents,
a blue and white flowered urn,
on her dark gleaming table.
For ten months, it peeks behind
pink and white carnations, old photos
of him at various ages I never knew
—four-year-old cowboy,
teenage Don Juan in bow tie,
suave, twentysomething entrepreneur
in white suit. Next comes the task
of deciding what to do with the ashes.

Spread them by plane over Lake Ontario?
Scatter them on the lawn of his old
school? Finally, after weeks
of deliberating, his mother says
we'll take them out East to her home town.
The day we bury the ashes,
a year after his death,
a hot wind hushes through the trees
calling him home

Blessings

That last afternoon
I saw him alive and still speaking
in the room over the Hudson
I lingered by his bed
pinning the red tube from his neck
to his striped cotton gown
and he said "God bless you"
eyes still waters
where I floated lightly
for a moment replying
"God bless you too"
in the deepening silence
the curl of his smile widening
as I heard him say,
"She already has, in so many ways"

Descent: Crossing the Dream

i

In the night I slip through dark lacy trees and beyond them the black mouth of rock before it is too late. Nothing but a flicker of light far down through darkness to the place where a woman sits in a sea of light. I see only this light till the woman smiles as though she knows me, eyes no hint of color, no centre point in the flames as she speaks: "Ah, you've come at last. What do you want?" I've come to grieve my lover, no more of my world, I tell her. What shall I do? "If grieving is your wish, grieving is what you'll have," she says waving hands toward two figures in the shadows. "Follow them." The figures lean into the black void, feet scraping stone till the air is damp with sea. We climb into a boat, travel days to rocky shores

ii

Silence but for slow footsteps toward me. Dark figures take my shirt, pants and underwear, no shoes but dirty socks. I stand naked before a stone gate, hand over a belly aching too much, the nights and days merging into one, memories locked in, hand on skin between thighs, grassy hills where we found an eagle feather over blue waters, too much to hold, everything different now but I can't see their faces, only their hands pointing to the gate

iii

Everything is hard here in this place of stone and sand. Nothing grows. Today the figures cleave long strands of my hair. Brown heap on the ground. All that's left of his fingers combing my hair, touching secrets he did not understand in the night nor could he carry alone, memories embedded in hair, his scent, all that he was and could be now lost, all that gone as I step through the second gate into grey morning air

iv

I hide in the shadows from the dark ones who gather stones down below, my skin ashen like everything around me. Alone and now not alone as the figures stand solemnly before me: "Come, it is time for the third gate," they say. "For this you must give us something you covet most of all." There is nothing left to give I say, but they step closer and before I can reach out my eyes burn and I fall into darkness, silent womb, infinite night

V

We walk for hours stopping to rest briefly on the stones, grass crackling under my feet. The world has left me, but I must still find my way, vision turned inward to the bones where his face is etched in a thousand places. Blood flows to my legs moving upward with the figures till they stop. "This is the fourth gate," they say. "What more have you to give us?" Nothing, I tell them, I have given too much. I drift into the other realm, nothing to show where I am or where I'm going, stillness holding me in its amorphous grip till voices press in my ears: "We will take your hands," then the sound of metal on bone. I am lost in the bruise of night

vi

My body is a hollow reed that remembers nothing, not even his face lost in the past though I walk through the valley of the shadow of death and feel nothing of what was before for nothing exists as it was, not of this body at least, stripped of hair, eyes and hands and even today as I stand at the fifth gate and they ask me to give more, I stare at them blindly for I do not see them, nor myself and even as they slice off my feet I care little of this charade, this circus of death, the death of the body that is, the veil we wear for so many years until we reach into the lace of stars

vii

What do I know but this slow release into darkness, this silence broken only by the sound of wings. My body is a shell of wounds I'm falling into but something beckons in the stillness. The figures have come again, this time lifting me on a cloth where I sway as we rise up the mountain. It is cooler here, with soft mists enfolding us, then moving off into the valley. The figures set me down, my body bending into the earth without a will of its own. A hand opens my mouth; cold on tongue till I taste only blood

viii

Echo of wings, closer. We are rising higher into the black hood of sky. I sway as the dark ones pass through the last gate then set me down on stone, cold on my bare skin. I am half here, half of the other world where light and shadow merge into pale greyness. The silence grows in hissing waves till the wings come again, ominous now, circling above, the eye of a storm. I know what the birds want and I'm ready to let them take this body where I have grown into stillness even as every part of me is taken away

ix

My skin cracks, my flesh rots, my bones dry out. Only the mourning doves visit my deathbed gathering each day at dawn grey wings hovering above me. After forty days the doves drop seeds into my bones. The seeds grow into blood and flesh, arms and legs. They grow into a new heart, a skull spinning strands of silky hair. The doves peck through rope around my waist and I follow them down the mountain. The boat is waiting. I climb in, begin the journey home

The Birthday

The day you turned thirty-five
a face of teeth smiling for the camera
your reed body tall above my mother
and sister beside me
sun soft in your eyes
nothing could stop us believing
the gods had pulled the black roots
from your spine,
that you'd slipped
through the crack of death.
Today waking to July's sultry embrace
words growing wide on the page
like the green maple hands
outside reaching for the light
my fingers press into patience
that some sign will come from you.
Late afternoon
hands deep in black earth
planting sunflowers
for your thirty-seventh year, the sun
burns away all the clouds—
a blue sky reigns

Conversations with a Dead Man

Why did you go?
What was here for me but pain. I lost my way.
My sorrow took me through the door.
Why did you go?
I don't know. It seemed right. The lights were
dimming and I had to follow.
Why did you go?
There was not enough for me here. I finished my work.
Why did you go?
I needed space. The rooms were dark. I couldn't breathe.
Why did you go?
I needed you. That scared me.
Why did you go?
The sun rose in another place, not here. I could see it
glowing. I wanted to follow it.
When will you be back?
When you call me. Speak the words.
When will you be back?
Birthdays, Christmas. When the space is set for me.
When will you be back?
Forever. I am here always.
Where did you go?
The place between places. The place of all silence.
Where did you go?
Into blue air. I am floating.
Where did you go?
Into stone, where we all rest

Letters From Him

i

Sometimes my longings are greater than I can feel
in this immense ocean of light.
Sometimes I fall on my phantom knees
and pray for simple pleasures
I did not understand:
the golden leaf falling slowly to the ground,
the single cloud billowing
through blue skies,
palms open to the sun's swell of warmth.
These are the moments I grow into now

ii

I waited for the rains to come.
I waited for the waters to wash away
all shadow, light.
Now I wait for nothing

Undeciphered Oracle

Overnight trees grow white veils—
every bough, leaf, bud
dawn's pearl light.
The darkest part of winter is yet to come,
spring is still so far off

*

Full moon weighted in a purple sky
wings fall from a tree,
a tiny bent body I reach out to hold
then stop—a voice inside saying
"All things die"

*

The eve of my fortieth year I'm alone in the dark
the room a chamber of shadows.
One candle quivers and in the light I see his face,
full and luminous.
My eyes drink him in till the dark
takes him back once again

*

The questions persist.
They grow like the small red buds on trees,
unseen under snow:
How can I navigate these long nights?
When will I love again?

*

Trees bow under the weight of snow,
blocking the path up the hill.
I shake their tangled branches loose
as twigs scatter into patterns on the ground:
morning's undeciphered oracle

*

Night: Coughing into the heat of my chest
I remember his last days, lungs swelling with liquid
the doctors didn't understand, even after his death.
Like the rest of us,
they travel blindly in the dark

*

Each day at the nursing home
my father opens his mouth
to the green mush they feed him
hoping to squeeze another day in his life.
In a few days he'll be married fifty years,
this anniversary his last gift to us—
or maybe he just can't let go

*

Thanksgiving, in brilliant light
pine trees dance
free now of snow

November, 1997
Stillwater, New York

LIGHT

Silence Gathering in Blue Air

What the heart remembers after years of absence:
a certain look in an old photo,
eyes brimming with dare and longing,
or the deep undercurrent of his voice
months later on a phone message never erased,
or mid-day on Palm Sunday along College Street
hand-in-hand on a crowded sidewalk after the second chemo,
but what of this light of morning in the long grass,
the soft trill of swallows, the gleam in the dark pond,
a solitary dragonfly stalking the garden
and what of the nights
silence gathering in blue air
a faint mist over the ridge of trees,
the cinders glowing amber in the darkened room.
It's taken eight years to learn
that death is not a failure
nor is it a bad dream we enter
when this world is lost to us.
We return to the beginning again,
where nothing matters but the heart
that continues its wild beat
searching for the skull of its birth,
wanting nothing but light

September, 2001
Salt Spring Island, B.C.

NOTES

"Descent: Crossing the Dream" uses elements of the ancient myth of Inanna, Queen of Heaven and Earth in Mesopotamia. In the myth, recorded on clay tablets and translated by Samuel Kramer (published in 1983 as *Inanna* by Kramer and Diane Wolkstein), Inanna descends to the underworld and passes through seven gates shedding a part of her regalia at each one. She is left to die, but is later reborn, symbolizing an archetypal journey of transformation experienced in all cultures. In part "v" of the same poem, "inward to the bones" is a line from Kate Braid

ACKNOWLEDGEMENTS

I would like to thank my mother, Mary, for her unwavering support over many years, as well as my sister Judy, and brothers Ken, Dave and Richard. My thanks, too, to May Doherty who shared the journey gracefully, Eugene Sunday, Paul Crampton, Rita Wyczynski, Phil and Claire Taylor, Bud and Lynn Collins, Lee Crawford, Bernadette Hardaker, Mark David Gerson, Mary Curtin and Bea Donald. I'm also deeply appreciative of my partner, Phil Goodger, for his support during the final stages of this manuscript.

I am thankful for financial assistance from the Toronto Arts Council, Canada Council and the Ontario Arts Council, which allowed me time to work on the collection, as well as The Banff Centre for the Arts and The Saskatchewan Artists/Writers' Colony for providing the space.

Credit is due to Libby Scheier, Marg Webb and Rosemary Sullivan, who offered editorial comments at various stages of the manuscript, as well as Phyllis Webb for her encouragement.

Selections of the collection were shortlisted for the CBC-*Saturday Night* literary awards in 1997, as well as the Canadian League of Poet's chapbook contest in 2000.

AGMV Marquis
MEMBER OF SCABRINI MEDIA
Quebec, Canada
2002